the Mindset SHIFT

from Employee to

HOME BUSINESS ENTREPRENEUR

By Amanda Ollier

&

Chris and Susan Beesley

This book is also available as an eBook at most online retailers.

the Mindset SHIFT

"Most people will achieve their greatest success one step beyond what looked like their greatest failure"
Brian Tracy

"Be miserable. Or motivate yourself. Whatever has to be done, it's always your choice".
Dr. Wayne Dyer

"Fear is the tool of a man-made devil. Self-confident faith in one's self is both the man-made weapon which defeats this devil and the man-made tool which builds a triumphant life. And it is more than that. It is a link to the irresistible forces of the universe which stand behind a man who does not believe in failure and defeat as being anything but temporary experiences"
Napoleon Hill

Dedication

This book is not only dedicated to you, it was written for you.

Our intention in writing this book, is to give you all the encouragement and tools you need, to nurture the beliefs that will take you to the limits of your imagination and beyond.

"You become what you think about most" - The Secret

Acknowledgements

Thank you to everyone who has contributed to the creation of this book by giving us their valuable time, energy, inspiration and feedback. Thanks also for confirming to us that we were on the right track and creating something of real worth.

We appreciate you all!

the Mindset SHIFT

From Employee to

Home Business Entrepreneur

By Amanda Ollier

&

Chris and Susan Beesley

Contents

Foreword

Ultimately, the most important first step to success is a true belief that it can be achieved. Without it you will never take the action necessary to reach your goal.

What Amanda, Chris and Susan have created here is a no-nonsense guide for those seeking to create that belief in themselves.

They speak in a way that really hits home, makes complete sense and most importantly, results in those who learn from them having total belief in their ability to create their own success.

The true magic of Amanda, Chris and Susan lies in the fact that they are real.

Despite the success they have now achieved, they have not forgotten where they started and how it felt every step of the way. They still recall with absolute clarity how frightening and uncertain those first few steps might be, how intimidating making that leap to independence can appear, or how difficult it can be to get back up when things may not go as expected. They draw upon these experiences to steer you in a way that allows you to avoid the pitfalls, helping you to compress your time to success.

As you hold this book in your hands, know that an extraordinary journey awaits. You merely need to open yourself up to it, spread your wings and JUMP.

JUMP right in, right NOW, and don't hold back.

Amanda, Chris and Susan will guide you every step of the way with practical, proven and clear to understand instruction and guidance, so that you may one day enjoy the riches and success that they have worked so hard to make available to you through the pages that follow.

I wish you great joy and success – you deserve it, you have the very BEST to guide you and now is your time!

Lisa Grossmann
Multi-millionaire Home Business Entrepreneur
http://LearnWithLisaNow.com

Why Are You Here?

There are a number of things that may have brought you here today, but one thing is for sure. If you are reading this book, then you are thinking about changing your life. Why else would you be reading a book written to help you do precisely that?

It is likely, given the title, that you are also thinking about starting your own home business and as a result you will have a number of questions rumbling around in your mind.

Whilst we don't know exactly how you will phrase these questions, we can pretty much guarantee that they will boil down to two fundamental, key questions which are…

* Can I do it?

* Will it work for me?

We know this because we've been where you are and we've helped lots of other people in your position and everybody has these questions to begin with.

The great news is, the answer to both those questions is a resounding yes and as you read on, you'll become more and more aware of why that's so.

Take heart, you're not alone!

Your Journey Starts Here...

"Be married to the process and divorced from the result"

By the time you finish this book, you will be ready to make a life changing choice.

It may be a choice you are already aware of which has led you to this book, or it may be one you have until now quietly ignored through fear or ignorance.

Either way, by the time you have read what we are going to share with you here, you will no longer be able to hide from that choice. It will be laid bare before you and from that moment on, your life will change as a result.

Whether that change is a good one or not will depend on you. We can't choose for you, neither can we say in advance which way you will decide to go.

All we can do is show you the roads that we have taken and arm you with the tools to start your own journey with the best possible chance of success.

The rest is down to you.

Just as it always is, always was and always will be.

Tips for the Road

Any road trip needs a bit of planning and preparation if it is to be a success, rather than one of those popular disaster or comedy movies, and your journey from being in the mindset of an employee to that of a home business entrepreneur is no different.

It's the rule of the 7 Ps

Proper

Prior

Planning

Prevents

Pitiful ;-)

Poor

Performance

Whilst we can't come with you physically on your journey, we can help you prepare!

Reading this book will be a great start. It will help you begin to scope out where your ideal destination is and map out the best road to get you there.

Just reading is only the start though. Reading gives you knowledge, but its applying that knowledge that will give you experience and wisdom.

We've included lots of exercises which will help you take the knowledge you gain and build it into something much more powerful and practical. Do them!

Get yourself a nice journal to record your thoughts as you go, and write down the answers to the exercises. If you're anything like Amanda, you won't need any more excuse to go and buy some new stationary, but if you need more of a reason, then it'll be a powerful reminder of how far you've come, when you look back, where you are going and most importantly why the journey is worth every step.

When you come to a part which really resonates with you, write it down. If you're reading this in paperback, we've left plenty of room in the margins, better still copy it into your journal, so that you can look back at it later and see your progress.

If you're reading this on an eReader like a Kindle or an iPad, you can use the built in facilities to make notes and highlight bits too.

Writing things down helps clarify them. Only thinking about something allows your mind to drift from one thing to another and you can lose focus without ever really answering the first question. If you have to write it down, you have to think it through to a logical conclusion.

Committing something to paper has the added benefit of creating a physical thing from your thoughts, which creates a vibration in tune with that thing. If you understand a little about the universal law of attraction, you will know that what you focus on and create energy about is ultimately what you will attract into your life.

As Napoleon Hill, author of the famous book Think and Grow Rich said

"Thoughts become things!"

So, read it, write about it, do the exercises and think about it all the time!

The Mindset Shift isn't a switch. We aren't going to give you a magic number to call, a button to press, or a pill to swallow, that will suddenly give you the mindset of a home business entrepreneur.

The Mindset Shift is a process. One which will take time and thought, and above all commitment.

Some days it will seem easy and you'll get it completely. On other days, it will seem nebulous and difficult to grasp and perhaps even hopeless. But every day that you read, and think, and make those all important little changes in your thought processes, you will get closer to making the Mindset Shift.

In many ways this is no different to any other area of life. Take your current job or business. Do you hand on heart enjoy that every day? Are some days harder than others? Do you leap out of bed every morning and think, 'Yippee! I get to go to work today!' Probably not!

Your new business will be no different. Some days will be better than others because that's the ebb and flow of life. Just be aware of that and avoid the temptation of blaming that on your business, of allowing doubt about your decision to change to creep in, or of allowing others to use that as an indicator that you've made a mistake. Hang in there!

The down days will help you to appreciate the up days more, and you'll soon come to recognise that those down days are usually a sign that you're about to breakthrough another barrier and reach a new all time high. You may even find yourself welcoming those not so good days, and enjoying them like you did the last week at school before the holidays.

Nothing in life worth having comes without effort and challenge of some kind. Nothing. This is no different, but boy is it worth it!

Who Are We?

Amanda Ollier

I am… how should I finish that sentence I wonder? I always find it tricky when trying to describe myself on paper. What to put in, what to leave out? Particularly when I'm writing something I hope will encourage you to think about yourself in new ways and with new definitions.

I am lots of things; some more relevant to you than others!

I am younger in my mind than my body – which I consider to be a good thing.

I am passionate about helping you to get the most out of your life that you can, by empowering you to make the mindset shift that you need to get you there.

I am a person who loves to love. Has an absolute abhorrence of lies and truthfully, just wants to make the world a better place. It's taken me a long time to admit that! Seems an odd thing to have spent most of my life trying to deny when I think about it, and every time I say it, it's like breathing out properly. My name is Amanda and I'm a dreamer and I want the world to live in peace and harmony. Surely that's a good thing isn't it?

I am also a woman – yes you may have guessed that from my name – and very proud of it. Like the beautiful rose has it's thorns to protect it, I believe that we women have a similar strength within our beauty and whilst I would never wish to live a life without men, I'm very glad that I'm a woman - not least because that has enabled me to be the mother of two wonderful boys who are my best work to date and the reason I am still young at heart. They are my why, my motivation and my purpose. I want to show my children, by my own example, what I believe to be true; that we are all responsible for our own lives and the creator of our own destinies. That with application and above all belief, we can achieve just about anything and that it is important to be honest and thoughtful.

I also want to show them that anyone can be successful and to give them the freedom to live their dreams. I want in short to leave them with a legacy to be proud of and values that they'll carry in their hearts forever.

On a more tangible note, I am a Master Practitioner of NLP (neuro-linguistic programming), Time Line Therapy™ and Hypnosis (so never look directly into my eyes!) a passionate coach, blogger and author of a series of self help books I call 'The Self Help Bible'.

I used to be a full time employee but decided to make the mindset shift myself in 2009. I didn't know at the time that that's what I was doing exactly and would, with hindsight, have benefited from a bit more planning of 'what next'. That said, I would not have had the journey that has led me here perhaps, had I done things differently. Everything happens for a purpose I believe. Don't you?

My desire now, is to help you build the life of your dreams, by living my dream of being a writer. So if this is the first time you've read me, I hope you enjoy and find value in what you find here and I hope you feel empowered to change your life for the better as a result. If just one thing makes you think a little differently, makes you do just one thing differently, who knows how far those ripples in the pond will reach?

***

I have known Chris and Susan since I began my own entrepreneurial journey a few years ago and so am delighted to be creating this book with them. They have shown me nothing but genuine kindness in the time I have known them and I am delighted to see them finally achieve the huge levels of recognition and success they deserve.

We are all passionate proponents and students of self development and so this book is a natural coming together of like minds, created from the genuine desire to help you help yourself.

I hope that we will succeed in lighting the touch paper for you and instilling in you, the confidence that you absolutely can succeed and have the life you desire and deserve.

Who Are We?

Chris and Susan Beesley

We are ... well the 'older generation' for want of a better word. Mature is probably better... and life is just beginning for us which is fantastic!

What's more, we are passionate about empowering you to make the mindset shift that you need to get the most out of life as well.

As a husband and wife partnership and a business partnership we really do have the best of both worlds and because of that we each have unique skills that have transformed our life and our business.

We are blessed to have five adult children and one grandchild - and now that the children have 'flown the nest' we have the time to fulfil our dreams in what we consider to be the best time in anyone's life.

We are accountants by profession and up until 2009 we were full time running our accountancy and management consultancy practice - working crazy hours and never finding any time to do the things we loved - like skiing and travelling the world.

We now 'work' full time online where we can continue our passion for coaching and training but with individuals like you ... and we can do that whilst pursuing our passion for travel because our business allows us to work from anywhere in the world where there's an internet connection ... including the ski slopes!

Did we have to go through a mindset shift to do this? Absolutely we did! Having a traditional business was realistically the same as having a job - being an employee of our own business, dictated to by our clients and the projects we had to manage for them.

And, as we said earlier we are a little older than most people who choose to make a change in their life (Susan refers to us as "no spring chickens") but we want to show you that anything is possible if you really want it enough.

***

We first met Amanda when she contacted us for some help with her online business and became one of our first coaching students. We quickly discovered that her passion was for personal development (the same as us) and that her passion wasn't an online business as she first thought but as an author and a proponent of NLP. She has since gone on to write a series of self help books - The Self Help Bible and dedicates her time and skills to helping children to read through her NLP skills.

Not only have we become firm friends, but share a common passion for helping anyone with a yearning to become a home based entrepreneur to make that shift

Now it's over to you...

Who Are You?

We know that what we are writing here will be relevant to lots of different people, all of whom have their own unique circumstances, just like you do. We also know from experience that only some of those who read this will succeed and that the degree of your success will depend almost entirely on you. Accepting that fact, is one of the first steps in becoming successful at anything and never more true than if you want to become a successful home business entrepreneur.

If you are not prepared to take the responsibility for your future, to be accountable to yourself without recourse to policies, bosses and other external crutches, you won't succeed. It's as simple as that!

Our way of life in the developed world has evolved to respond to and cater for our needs over time and in some regards it has almost gone full circle. Our jobs are so demanding that the things we once went to work for, are now almost lost in the mists of our minds. As work has become less about survival in a primal way, our expectations of what our jobs should provide for us have grown and this means that we then need to earn more money to fulfil those desires.

More money usually means more time and energy spent at work, which leaves less to spend at home, doing the things we want to, with the people we love and went to work to support in the first place. It's a vicious circle.

We want more, so we have to give more, which means we have less than we started with.

Not much of a trade when you look at it like that is it?

Our upbringing and schooling lead us in this direction. We, our parents, peers and society at large, are all operating within this same framework where established norms are accepted and expected.

In many ways, this kind of normalisation is a good thing. Our world is densely populated and if we did not have a set of widely accepted constraints on our behaviour, we could not peacefully co-exist in large societies. For many people, the life we are taught to expect – working for someone else our entire adult life in the hope of a reasonable pension upon retirement – is perfectly acceptable.

For some however, it is not, and if you are reading this book, it is highly likely that you are one of an increasing number of people who are no longer prepared to accept this model without question.

You may be a professional person, looking for a change of career to replace or subsidise your income. Perhaps you are one of the growing number of people affected by the recession and you need an alternative; a new plan B.

Perhaps you are just sick of your current situation and looking for anything which is not that, or maybe your motivation is about having more than you currently have. Maybe you are dissatisfied with your current lifestyle and want to have more of the good things in life or just to regain some sense of control.

Are you a parent who wants to spend more time being a parent and less time being an employee?

Or do you feel unfulfilled and know that you have more to offer than you currently are and want a forum to do it through?

There are any number of reasons why you might have chosen to read this now, rather than at any other time. We could go on listing reasons all day. The bottom line is, you want a change. You are at the very least curious about trying your hand at something else and to start with that curiosity is enough. Like the key ingredient for a delicious recipe, curiosity is the first indicator of change. So if you are curious, great! Embrace that curiosity, feed it and let it grow into the compulsion to dare to go out and change your life!

Many of the people who read this will have never tried their hand at anything but being an employee; a conventional J.O.B. It's what we're brought up and schooled to do, what most of us believe our working life will consist of from the earliest age

You may have tried other options but given up before you made it, or just not had the success you hoped for.

In any event, it doesn't matter what's gone before, or where you've been. It doesn't matter if you've tried and failed or never even tired. All that matters is what you do from here on in.

Whether you want to make a little additional money each month, to replace your salary, or earn so much money you'll look back and wonder how you survived on your current income, it's all possible.

It's all possible if you want it to be and are prepared to do what needs to be done to make it so.

We are fortunate in that we live in an age where it is acceptable to question and explore alternatives and to choose our own destiny - even if it still takes a bit of courage to do so!

You may have to learn to overcome (or ignore) the prejudice of others, find yourself ostracised or humoured and walk this pathway alone at times, but you do have the possibility to do things differently if you wish to.

Your current mindset - your way of thinking, your beliefs and attitudes, values and experiences, the choices you have made to date - have created the life that you currently have.

In order to change your life, you will have to begin by making a shift in your mindset.

You cannot achieve success in any area of your life without doing it in your mind first.

Unless you wish to do something totally outlandish or innovative, there are people who have already accomplished what you now want to, so you know it is possible. Success leaves a trail and you can easily tap into the learnings and systems of these successful people should you wish to. That's the easy part.

The hard part is first persuading every cell in your body that you really do want to leave the relative safety of your comfort zone and carve out a new pathway for yourself.

If you are to be successful, and by this we mean achieve a life beyond even that magical one you have until now only glimpsed in dreams, you are going to have to step beyond your warm and quilted comfort zone and into the less certain but more fertile growth zone. Without growth, you will at best, stay exactly where you are.

Don't misunderstand us, you may have a perfectly satisfactory life right now, but if you want MORE and BETTER, you will need to change and grow.

And when you cross that line, your courage in both hands, as you begin this growth, the unconscious part of you that wants to maintain the status quo and keep you within the relative safety of your comfort zone is going to put up the fight of its life!

It is going to use every weapon at its disposal to keep you where you are. To keep you safe, because that's it's job - and it does it very efficiently!

Your unconscious is going to tune you into every word of caution counselling you to, 'Stop being so stupid' and 'get back to reality'. To 'Be grateful for what you've got rather than looking for something that might not exist', to 'stick to what you know' etc

It is going to highlight all the examples of others who have tried and failed and the things you already have and should be thankful for.

It is going to help you notice tons of evidence to make you think that you can't succeed in new ways.

It's going to throw the 'F' word at you in as many forms as it can find.

It is going to amplify your feelings of FEAR.

* Fear of impending failure

* Fear of disappointing those who love and look up to you

* Fear of not proving those who expect you to fail wrong

* Fear of this being another 'harebrained scheme that didn't work out' –

* Fear that the fantastic life that you have allowed yourself to imagine, the wonderfully compelling goals that you have dared to set yourself and the ultimate version of yourself that you have created in your minds-eye, don't already exist right now.

* Fear that the doubters and hope-busters who said that you had to work hard all your life to get by; that you would never amount to much because successful people aren't like you, they're born different - were right.

* Fear you'll be 'taken in', 'had', or 'conned'

* Fear that you'll be successful. If it's new territory to you, as much as you want it, it can be terrifying.

And that's only the things that you're going to come up with yourself!

Imagine what Mr Moody and Little Miss Doubtful will be able to contribute to that list!

BUT STOP!

It doesn't have to be like that!

We are here to reassure you, that it's only your mindset that stands between you and your life as it is in the present moment and the life you see when you dare to dream those magnificent dreams. Through the course of this book, we will show you why that is and how you can prove it.

We will show you how to make the mindset shift.

The shift from being an employee to a home business entrepreneur.

We will tell you what you need to know and give you the questions that you need to ask yourself to find the answers that are right for you.

For now, you just need to know that working 40 or 50 or more hours a week to just *get by*, is **only one option.**

Listening to people who do not have the success you want or the passion to achieve it, is **only one option.**

Trading your time for money and having more month than money, is **only one option.**

Going without, so that your loved ones don't have to; skipping holidays, outings, maybe even meals, is **only one option.**

It may currently seem like your only option, but it is still ONLY ONE OPTION.

Sticking with what you know and what you've done, will never get you further than you've already come. **But it is not your only option.**

If you are serious about creating the life of your dreams, of becoming the most perfect version of you that it's possible to be, of having the freedom to spend your time how and with who you want to, of doing exactly as you please, of stepping out from the shadows of employment and into the light of entrepreneurialism

AND

If you are prepared to step outside of your comfort zone; to dare to dream and fight for your future, to work hard to make the mindset shift that will lead you to success, we are here to tell you that the perfect time is now!

The time is absolutely right for you to create the mindset, that will pull you headlong into that future at a speed and with a desire that you have yet to experience.

This is YOUR time.

The time for that doubting voice, those all consuming fears, the lack, the worry and the making do – **that time is over.**

Finished; Period.

Today is the first day of the rest and best of your life because you are going to make the mindset shift.

Common Fears and Misconceptions

Before we go any further, let's just talk about some of the misconceptions we've come across whilst mentoring others or on our own journeys shall we? Get them out into the open and dealt with in case any of them are trundling round in your head too.

Think back to a time when you didn't yet know how to do something that you do now. It might be something like driving a car, a skill that you developed for a job, or a hobby – anything that you learned to do.

Before you knew how to do it, you probably had an idea of what it might be like and how hard or easy it might be to master.

As you learned to do it you will have discovered how right or wrong you were and you may well have been surprised – pleasantly in some cases and not so much in others!

Becoming an entrepreneur is no different in some regards. You probably have an idea of some of the things you'll need to do and no clue about others.

The point is, that until you have done it, most of these ideas are only your preconceptions based on what you already know and things that other people have told you.

Many of them will be deeply unconscious and unfortunately have the power to prevent you from being successful.

Moving into new territory can be daunting and exciting in equal measures but because it is new, you will be missing some of the familiar checkpoints and measures you would usually gauge your experiences on. You are operating in the growth zone, beyond your comfort zone and remember, that's a good thing! The feeling of learning new skills and ways of doing things can be exhilarating if you let it.

Here are some of the very common misconceptions and limiting beliefs we have encountered (and even held ourselves at some point). See if any of them apply to you. Read the list slowly and see if any of them seem silly or appropriate to you. Trust your inner compass to guide you. Make a note of those that you feel might be true, you'll need to eradicate them later and if any others pop into your mind, make a note of them too.

* It doesn’t work

* It won't work for me

* It's too hard, I'm not techie. I can't do it

* I'm too late – I missed the boat

* The time's not right yet

* It's not for people like me

* It's easy and will happen overnight

* It costs a fortune and takes years to learn

* You can get systems where you just press a button and make loads of money for no effort

* I can't give up my job

* I can't be successful

* I don't deserve it

*I'm not good enough

Feel free to add your own to the list. We might not have put them here, but you can be pretty sure you won't be the first person to have had the thought. We'll look later at how to get rid of limiting and unhelpful thoughts like these so please do make a note of them now.

We cannot stress enough how important it is to know how you really think about this. Your underlying beliefs are so crucial in creating your future. If you don't believe you can be successful then you are right and nothing you do will change that unless you deal with that fundamental belief first. You will only ever be as successful as you believe you can be.

What Do You Want to Achieve?

"To ask, 'How do you do it?' is already starting off on the wrong foot. When reaching for the stars, there does not have to be a 'how' if there is a big enough 'why'." Criss Jami

Start With Your Why

To be successful in life you need a reason, an aim. Napoleon Hill called it the '**Definite Chief Aim**'.

When Alice asked the Chelsea Cat, during her adventures in Wonderland, if she was on the right road, he asked her where she was going. She said she didn't know and he replied that in that case any road would get her there! And he was right. If you are wandering aimlessly you will never arrive at your destination because you don't have one! You may miss golden opportunities because you don't appreciate their significance and you are likely to live in a perpetual state of dissatisfaction and feel unfulfilled.

If you are thinking about making the change from employment to being a home based entrepreneur, there must be a reason and the first step in your journey is to establish what that is.

This is your WHY.

* Why do you want that change?

* What are you looking for that you don't currently have in your life?

* What do you currently have in your life that you wish to eradicate or reduce?

To discover what your why is, you need to look beyond the obvious and material.

"Your future has absolutely nothing to do with your past. It has everything to do with what you are willing to do right now." Dave Sharpe, Co-Founder of Empower Network

Look for the end result, the emotional reward, the feeling that comes as a result of having that thing that first comes to mind and that's where you'll find the real reason why and the thing that will drive and motivate you.

All the things we yearn for in life, as practical and tangible as they might seem, ultimately lead to a positive feeling. We all want to improve our lives; to *feel better*.

When thinking about changing what you *do for a living* (now isn't that an interesting phrase in itself!) you may well want more money. You may have a long list of the things you'll buy with it and think that this is your reason why, but if you look at the list and ask yourself

* *Why do I want that?*

* *For what purpose?*

You will very quickly notice that owning those things is just a means to an emotional end. Either it will make you feel better about something or it will make someone you care about feel better.

Example

If one of the things you'd like to do is to buy a bigger house, think about what having that new house will give you? – space, relaxation and freedom perhaps? Imagine how you will feel when you are sitting inside it. What emotions and feelings spring to mind?

Would you like to take more holidays? If so, why? What will that do for you?

Maybe you'd like a newer or better car? What will getting that give you or conversely take away from you?

The key thing each time is that the money is <u>not</u> the motivation, it is just the vehicle to get what you want.

A financial means to achieving an emotional end.

Of course it doesn't all have to be about money. As we have already seen, your job represents so many different things for you and you may be seeking something entirely different. As ever, there are no right or wrong answers, go with what feels right for you.

There are four key questions you should be asking yourself when trying to establish what you want. **The 4 Key Power Questions**. These same questions can be adapted and used in any situation where you want to get to the truth at an unconscious level – either in yourself or in others.

They are derived from quantum linguistics and are invaluable! You can see an example of the Power Question Matrix below and download one from http://theselfhelpbible.com/resources/worksheets

The Power Question Matrix

What WILL happen if you DO	What WON'T happen if you DO
What WILL happen if you DON'T	**What WON'T happen if you DO**

These four simple questions allow you to see the problem/issue/question from all angles and challenge your unconscious to see that there are different ways to contemplate the issue. They are often hard to think about and answer – and that's great! The harder it is to find an answer, the deeper you are delving into the realm of your unconscious. The only thing is that you must think about them until you find an answer!

If something quickly pops into your head, then write that down too – no matter how trivial or silly it might seem. There are many reasons why your unconscious keeps things locked away and when it lets them through into your conscious awareness they may not make much sense to you. Just know that it is always deliberate and never random no matter how odd it might seem.

Write them down because this is where the real gold nuggets are to be found. The thoughts, feelings and fears that you've kept hidden from yourself are the barriers that have held you where you are. Getting them out into the open is the first step to getting rid of them. So please, don't filter, just record it all.

You may find that something you write now will not make sense to you for some time to come, but at some point, in the future as you look back to now, that eureka moment will arrive, when the last piece of the puzzle falls into place and the penny drops. Don't miss out on that satisfaction by trying to decide now what's important and relevant, just write it all!

Exercise

1) List the areas of your life that will be positively affected when you become a successful home business entrepreneur and write down why that will be of benefit to you and those you love.

2) Ask yourself why you want those things and what positive purpose they will fulfil and as always, <u>write down your answers</u>.

These two things will form the basis of some of the work you'll need to do to create your goal later. Enjoy taking time to make the picture you paint with your words as colourful as you can. Listen to the voice inside you that's been waiting to sing about that future and record all the wonderful components of it.

Get the F*** Out of Here!

When you face your fear, most of the time you will discover that it was not really such a big threat after all. We all need some form of deeply rooted, powerful motivation—it empowers us to overcome obstacles so we can live our dreams. —Les Brown

The F word; Fear; It plagues us all.

That list of fears we cited earlier are all too common and affect so much of our lives without us even being aware of them. Like all fears, they are deeply seated in the unconscious and often disguise themselves as helpful protectors. Unlike the more tangible things like the fear of death, public speaking and creepy-crawlies, we are often unaware of their origins and often even their existence.

Some fears need to be faced head on, whilst others require more delicate plans of attack. The important thing is to understand where they come from. The good news is that most of them are monsters of your own creation - and that's the bad news too!

That voice inside your head is the mother and father of your fears and until you make it change its tune, they will continue to exist. Tackling your self-talk, the things you say to yourself all day long, is a brilliant place to start.

Interestingly, you can often tell a lot about the origin of your fear by identifying that voice. Who does it sound like? Like someone from your past, a parent or authority figure perhaps? Or maybe it's your own voice with a particular tone – admonishing, mocking or warning or maybe one of caution and concern?

Exercise

This is a really simple one.

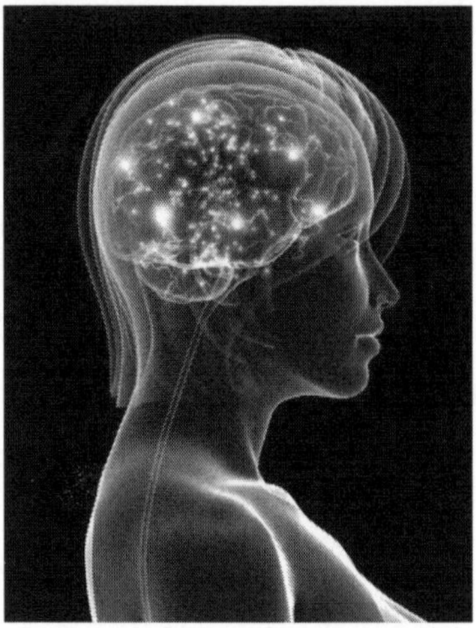

Listen to the voice inside your head and become your own censor. Do not allow yourself to say or think anything negative about anyone, and especially yourself.

If you can do this consistently for 10 days you will be amazed at the difference, not only to how you feel but also to how you behave and how others behave towards you.

If you find yourself thinking unkind things about someone else, force yourself to think of one nice thing to counteract it.

If you think something negative about yourself, find two things to replace it with – and make them different things each time! This will start to build you up a good list to use later when you have to assess your strengths too!

***

The thing is, that the majority of your fears will never ever actually happen, they are just figments of your imagination. You give them life by thinking about them and because of the way your mind works, you will find more and more things that make them appear real.

Your *'reality'* is created by a complex set of unconscious filters, which knock out the majority of what's around you without it ever getting as far as your conscious awareness. Of the two million bits of information that are picked up by your unconscious every second, about 7 (give or take a couple) actually make it through your filters. So if the filters are not set up to support the life you want to create, you just won't get the information you need, or the reality you want.

It's a bit like a sieve. If the holes in your sieve are big enough to allow pebbles through, you'll never catch the gold dust.

Two sets of filters that you will definitely need to work on in order to get the success you want, are your beliefs and your values. If they are out of alignment with what you want to achieve in life, you won't get it. It really is as simple as that!

You can find lots of information on the unconscious processes of your mind, the filters and how they help create your reality in Volume 3 of The Self Help Bible, we'll just look at beliefs and values here because they are the two most important areas.

If you believe that you will never be rich for example, or you had a value which said that money was evil, even if someone gave you lots of money you wouldn't keep it. You'd either give it away or lose it all. There are often stories in the media of people who win millions on the lottery and then a few years later find themselves destitute, just as there are those who seem to make money out of thin air. It all fits with what you fundamentally believe to be possible.

Be careful though as these beliefs are often very well camouflaged as something else. A very common scenario, is the person who gives away much of their fortune, thinking themselves to be the great philanthropist but still feels unhappy. Quite different to those who help others and feel fulfilled by it. The difference lies in the belief set that underpins the action. The first person is giving the money away to get rid of it, because they do not consider themselves to be deserving or worthy, or capable of success; the second is sharing their fortune in the belief that doing so will enhance their lives and fortunes. Whilst both may have a positive short term effect, the second will also have a longer term one for them.

Assessing your beliefs with regards to success and wealth is a key exercise and again an easy one to do.

Your beliefs, are basically generalisations about the world that you accept with conviction, as being true. They are created, for the most part, when you are quite young. Some you will adopt because they are taught or shown to you as being truths, some because of something you see, experience or think yourself. In either case, it is important to remember that your beliefs are only true if you want them to be.

At some point, you decided (unconsciously) that something was true for you and then, because of the way your unconscious works to support you, you acted as though that belief was true. This will in turn have given you more cause to believe that '**thing**' in the form of apparent evidence, and strengthened your conviction. Much like a snowball rolling down a hill, with time and accumulated experience, your belief will seem more and more real.

Positive beliefs can be empowering and increase your chances of success. Negative and limiting beliefs will at best restrict your achievements and at worst can really ruin your life.

If something doesn't support what you believe to be true, you won't pay as much attention to it, because your beliefs are so fundamental to you. They are like the framework or skeleton of your life. Your unconscious will simply delete things that don't match your beliefs before you are even aware of them.

If you had a belief about something and then never saw, heard or felt anything to support that belief, it would be pretty hard to continue to think the same way wouldn't it? So your unconscious will rank things which support your beliefs higher and you are more likely to notice them.

The problem with this is, as we have already mentioned, your beliefs are not empirical truths. They are just things that you have decided are true for you at an unconscious level.

Examples

Imagine that when you were young, you were frightened by a dog. You may well create an unconscious belief as a result, that all dogs are dangerous. This would happen to protect you – a very common reason for beliefs to be created – and you would likely grow up being afraid of dogs, even though you probably wouldn't remember that first incident. This doesn't mean that all dogs really are dangerous though does it? Your behaviour and attitude would make it seem so and you'd probably miss lots of chances to be proved wrong!

Another example. Imagine hearing your parents talk very disparagingly about rich people during your formative years, saying "*they're all greedy and make their money by ripping people off*". You would construct a belief, a generalisation, that all rich people were unpleasant, greedy con-men. Not only would it make you less likely to become rich, because your unconscious would want to avoid you becoming like those people and therefore help you avoid getting rich, but, because of the way your internal filtering system works, you wouldn't spot things to prove you wrong either. Your filters tune in to the things that match your beliefs and simply ignore the rest, so you'd never notice all the evidence around you to contradict them.

***

You will have taken on a lot of the beliefs of the people who brought you up and socialised with you when you were young. This will have helped you to fit into their world and create a safe zone for you to grow up in, but this has its own problems too.

* Whilst the belief might have worked for that person, it does not mean it is right for you too

* You may have been too young to make a proper evaluation of the facts or to explore other alternatives

* It may have worked for you at a certain point in your life but that doesn't mean it does now or will in the future

* As well as your own evolution, the world is also constantly changing and what stood true 20 years ago, for example, may no longer be so

Finding Your Octopus

Identifying Your Beliefs

As we have said, your beliefs are (unconsciously) your creation and therefore changeable – and quite easily too for the most part! They are not truths, so rather than thinking of them as being right and wrong or good and bad, think of them as either helpful or unhelpful.

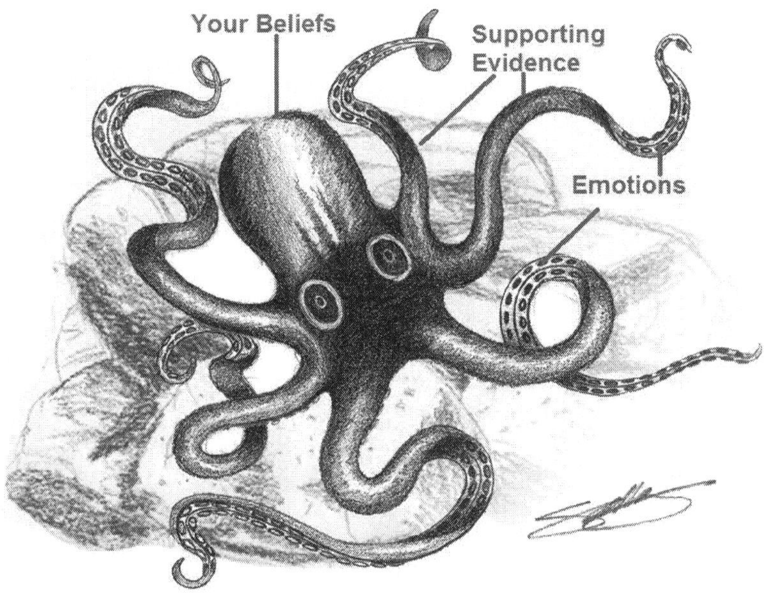

Think of your belief system as being like an octopus clinging to a rock. You have the body of the belief, which is held up by the legs – the evidence you've spotted to support your belief– and then you have the little suckers on the legs which stick it to the rock – these are the emotions and anchors you've created in relation to your belief.

In order to shift the octopus, you have to unstick its legs from the rock. To change a belief you have to identify the 'evidence' you've found and the emotional anchors you've created, and remove them. Then there is nothing to hold that belief to you any longer and you can replace it with something altogether more beneficial.

Exercise

The first task is to identify the octopus – the limiting belief.

An easy way to do this is to think about the thing that you hope to achieve and then work out why you don't already have it.

Some examples in relation to career success might be:

1) I want to be a successful home business entrepreneur

So the statement to explore is:

I can't be a successful home business entrepreneur because

2) I want to make more than $100,000 per year

And the statement would be

I can't make more than $100,000 because

Others are more straightforward, things like,

I'll never be rich because

I don't want to be rich because

I can't be successful because

Write down the statement at the top of a page and then begin writing down all the things that you can think of.

You may find strange things just pop into your mind and that's great. Just write them all down. Don't filter, just write.

The list you come up with will be the legs of the Octopus. All the reasons (evidence) as to why you cannot have, do or be the thing in the statement.

Of course they are not evidence in the true sense of the word. They are a collection of thoughts created out of FEAR, which we all know stands for **False Evidence Appearing Real**. That's how the Octopus hangs on so well, because he has so many legs! And your belief will be stronger the more reasons you can find to support it.

You might be surprised to find for example, that you think of rich people in a negative way –*they're selfish, arrogant, unhappy* - and you would only have to look in the press for a day to find examples where this appears to be true. If this is the case, is it any wonder that your unconscious has been saving you from wealth? Why would the thing designed to protect you and watch out for your best interests want you to become selfish, arrogant and unhappy?

Now as you look down that list, you are likely to recall certain situations and circumstances where your belief appeared to be real – where you saw the evidence – and as you recall those incidents you will perhaps remember how you felt. Did you suffer disappointment, guilt, embarrassment, humiliation? Did your pride take a knock or your confidence get squashed? Did you feel some kind of repulsion? Any of these sort of things will have created a negative emotional response in you and left an unpleasant feeling, and this is the sticky pads on the legs. You are anchored by the feelings created by your fear to these beliefs, just as the Octopus uses his little suckers to cling to the rock!

Getting the Octopus off the Rock

Changing Limiting Beliefs

"Most real failures are due to limitations which men set upon their own minds" Napoleon Hill in Outwitting The Devil

Now comes the most important part. Once you have identified the beliefs that feel like the most damaging and relevant to you, you need to come up with a more empowering alternative to replace them with. It's no use just thinking "That's stupid I'm not going to believe that anymore." This process is simple, but not quite that simple! Remember these beliefs have been created and reinforced over time because you have used them repeatedly and so unless you replace them with something different, you will default to what you know.

It's like walking to work each day, taking the same path every time. If you were suddenly told you couldn't go that way anymore, you'd have to find an alternative wouldn't you? And if you couldn't find one easily that met your needs, you'd just stick to the route you knew. That's exactly how your unconscious will work. It likes the path of least effort!

Begin to think about what you would like the belief to be. Going back to our two examples, we might pick something like "*I am a successful home business entrepreneur*" and "*I make more than $100,000 a year easily and happily*". You write whatever feels right for you.

Next think about evidence to support that. Look at the old belief and the list of evidence you drew up and start to pull it apart.

If you have something like

"*I am not good enough*"

Find examples of times when that wasn't true, when you were good enough. Ask yourself if that is really true all the time.

For example, if you wrote down

"I can't be successful because I never finish things off"

Then you need to find examples of times where you did finish things well.

If you wrote

"I don't want to be rich because my family won't like it"

Think of lots of reasons why your family will like it, something else you've done that they didn't like at first perhaps and also reasons why you don't have to build your life around what anybody else thinks.

Attack the problem from every angle. Up until now you have only seen it from your habitual perspective. Just acknowledging that there may be another way to see it is a huge step.

Is there anything on your list that is such a show stopper that you should let it stand in the way of your dreams? Probably not!

Ask yourself things like

* Is this always true, or can I think of times when it wasn't?

* Is this true for everyone or are there exceptions?

* What could I change so that this would no longer worry me?

* To what extent does thinking this help me?

* What would be a better, more empowering way to see this?

* How sensible would this sound if I said it in Mickey Mouse's voice?

* How likely is this to actually happen?

Once again, write it down!

Every reason that you can find, every counter argument, every alternative point of view helps diminish your fear. You are making your mind think about it in a different way, to consider the alternatives and you'll be surprised at how effective this exercise alone is at changing the way you think about things.

Are there things that make you feel a bit uncomfortable when you try to imagine what it would feel like if they weren't true? Probably!

If you've convinced yourself that something is stopping you getting what you want – an inherent deficiency in yourself, your upbringing, your social circle, your education, something that happened to you etc and suddenly you are thinking about denying that thought any more power, by taking responsibility and looking for an alternative, you can and should expect to feel at least uncomfortable! In fact, the worse you feel, the better it is! Those feelings are a real sign that you are making change, or at least room for change, at a deeply unconscious level, so stick with it.

Look at those legs from every possible angle to see why they are not truths until they just can't hold up that belief any more.

Use the four questions we told you about in the section on **The Power Question Matrix** on page 47/48 and try to imagine their opposite being true. Think about what is actually at their root. You'll usually find a hidden fear of something lurking there.

As with any unconscious change, the exploration is the most important part. Questioning what you have hitherto accepted as a truth is often enough to smash it. There are lots of other things you can do to cement the changes you wish to make and you will find some suggestions in the next section on Values, another equally significant factor.

But before that…

As you are reading this go back to a time in your life when you just believed. I know there was a time in your life when you believed in something; it may not have made sense to others, but it made sense to you. The fire inside of you spoke out to you and whispered:

"This is where you need to be. You are in the right place, right here, right now."

Maybe it was when you met your wife or husband. Perhaps it was a magical moment when you made a decision "now" and it impacted your life forever. It could even be a time when you had that tiny grain of faith that has the power to move mountains.

Take that power into the present moment, and harness the power of belief.

It is this seemingly magical power that will drive you past obstacles like they don't exist. You must see in your mind what is going to happen before it happens. It all starts with belief.

DECIDE to believe.

DECIDE to take action.

BELIEVE that what has worked for others can and will work for you.

You have the power within yourself to bend your universe and create a life that makes the fairy tales wish that they were you.

Thanks to Dave Wood, co-founder of the Empower Network for that inspiring suggestion!

Values

"Your beliefs become your thoughts. Your thoughts become your words. Your words become your actions. Your actions become your habits. Your habits become your values. Your values become your Destiny" Mahatma Gandhi

Values are another set of deeply unconscious filters that help create your perception of the world. Unlike beliefs which are wide ranging generalisations, values are used to help you measure or evaluate things. They are shaped through your experiences and are the things that let you know what's right and wrong, or good and bad. They are made to support your beliefs and are the ground-rules or standards you set for your life. They decide what you will spend time and energy on; what you are prepared to fight for.

They will help determine how you feel about your own actions and those of others. If you have behaved in a way that compromises one of your values, you will feel uncomfortable with your action. You might describe it as an act that is '*out of character*,' which basically means you've stepped outside of your usual value set.

Values have both a hierarchy or rank, and a direction. Hierarchically, the most important ones at the top of the list will easily outweigh those further down. When there is any conflict you will act in support of the one higher up the tree. So if money is higher up the tree than honesty for you, you won't have any problem conscience wise in getting money by less than honest means!

In some cases the value will be created to help you avoid something, in other cases it will be to enable you to move towards or achieve it and two seemingly opposing values might have the same aim.

We can explain this better with an example. Let's look at your financial values and how you might feel or think about wealth. You may have a value which encourages you to avoid or move away from poverty, and in moving away from poverty, you will accumulate more wealth. Or, you may have a value which motivates you towards being richer.

Whether you are moving away from being poor or towards being rich, your direction of travel is the same. What is not the same however; the difference that makes the difference, is your motivation and focus.

One value is motivated by fear and the compulsion to avoid the thing you are focusing on (in this example being poor) and the closer you are to reaching destitution, the stronger your motivation to move away will be.

The other value is motivated by more positive emotions, like desire, comfort, satisfaction, security etc and you will be more motivated the closer you get to your goal, so that the momentum will literally pull you along! You can be successful with either direction of travel, but you will enjoy the journey more if you are working towards the thing you want, rather than running from the fear of its opposite.

This is also how the **law of attraction** works, by presenting you with things that match your focus. So if you want to move away from something you fear, it's that fearful thing that you'll be thinking about and the law of attraction will give you more of that thing. It can't do otherwise because it is an immutable law. Things attract other things like themselves. Your unconscious, will filter things in and out of your conscious awareness according to how they fit in with your values. This helps maintain the appearance that your values are true. But like your beliefs, they are only true for you if you choose them to be.

You can easily see why it is beneficial to you to work on your values to make them more positive can't you! As well as the frame of mind they create, the closer you get, the faster you'll go! Isn't that great!

Identifying a value that would serve you better if it was more positive is very simple. Here's a really easy way to start the process.

This will work in any area of your life, but here we are going to focus on your career and the values you have associated with it.

"It's not hard to make decisions when you know what your values are" Roy Disney (The Art of Disney)

Exercise

Begin by asking yourself if you are where you want to be in that area.

* *Do I have the career I would ideally like?*

* *Am I in my perfect job?*

* *Does my job fit me and my life?*

There are no right or wrong questions here, use what works best for you.

When you hit a 'no', take a sheet of paper and begin writing a list of the things that are important to you in relation to this area.

Write a long list of words. No sentences, no waffle, just a list of words. Keep going until you can't think of any more. Don't filter the list, just allow your mind to give you what it wants to and write down exactly what comes into your head.

Keep saying to yourself,

"What's important to me in the context of my job?"

and write down what pops into your head.

When you can't think of anything else that is important to you in the context you are thinking about (career for now), stop. You should be aiming for a list of at least 50, but keep going until you really can't think of any more, as the best ones will often come after you would first have stopped. This is when the conscious mind switches off and leaves the unconscious to give the best answers!

You might like to use the following list as a starter but it is by no means exhaustive or correct. You might feel that two things we have written mean the same thing for you and that's fine. Or you may look and think '*That's got nothing to do with my job*' and that's fine too!

When you can't think of anything else that is important to you in the context you are thinking about (career for now) stop.

Next, read through the list and decide which are the 10 most important out of that list. Remember, there is no judgement involved here, no right or wrong and don't spend too long thinking about it. Just go with your gut instinct about what feels most important. Listen to the voice in your head, which will guide you if you listen and go with the words that look and sound right to you.

If you find it hard choosing between some of them, ask yourself '*Is A more important than B?*' or '*If I had A but not B would that be ok?*'

When you have your top 10, write them down on another piece of paper, divided into 3 columns. You can find a readymade template of the value elicitation table at

http://theselfhelpbible.com/resources/worksheets if you would like one.

For the second column, you need to ask yourself, is this value driving me away from something I don't want, or towards what I do want? Write down a 'T' if you are going towards the positive and 'A' if you are moving away from something undesirable.

Now look at your list. Is it mainly 'A', or mainly 'T'? Does that reflect your thoughts and feelings in relation to this area of your life? Do you see your current job as a way of moving you towards the things you want or keeping you from the things you fear?

Can you spot any patterns which match this in your life?

For example, if you are mostly 'A's you may find that you're really good at starting things, but not so great at finishing things off. This is because the further you get from what you don't want – the thing you're trying to avoid – the less motivated you'll be. The distance fools you into a false sense of security. You may also find that when things are going well, that some kind of crisis will arise and you'll end up back where you were.

This is a good example of how your unconscious and the universal law of attraction work. Your mind and your focus are on the thing you don't want, so your vibrational energy is at the frequency of that thing. The law of attraction works by giving you the thing that matches your frequency, so if your focus is on what you don't want, that's what you get more of! The reason it seems like you work best when under pressure is that your motivation is at its strongest when you are close to that thing you are trying to avoid. So, one crisis later and you're back in the best place to get you really motivated!

If you are operating this kind of strategy, you might find yourself thinking or saying something like 'I work best under pressure,' or 'I thrive on stress.' Of course, this is nonsense! Stress is not good for your body, it's just that you feel exhilarated by your fear of that 'thing' – being poor, being made redundant, having another failed relationship etc The feeling of exhilaration is just a physical reaction to the adrenalin pumping round your body, activated by your primal instinct of fight or flight.

If you are more 'T' than 'A', you might find it hard to get going, but your motivation will increase the closer you get to your goal. It's hard to get started because the end seems so far away and unlikely. You'll speed up and get more enthusiastic the closer you get because your focus is towards the thing you desire. You can easily get round this by creating lots of milestones on the way to your end goal, so that you always know what's next to keep you moving forward.

This part of the exercise alone may be enough to help you refocus your intention and understand why you are not always achieving what you want to. If you pay attention, you will become aware of your behavioural tendencies, which will leave enough of a gap for you to jump in and spot a more beneficial behaviour or reaction. Habits are created through repetition, nothing more. They become automatic because we do them over and over again until we can do them without the need for conscious thought. It doesn't mean they are permanent patterns and you can easily change them with a bit of consistent conscious action. If you do something consistently for just 10 days, you will have broken the boundaries of even the most stubborn habit and made room for a new more empowering replacement.

If you would like to take it a step further and change some of your values to make them more compelling, there are a number of ways you can do this.

Subliminal messaging and hypnosis are two great tools for changing beliefs and the values created to support them. Daily affirmations will help too, as will creating a dream board to aid effective visualisation. The effectiveness of all these tools is largely due to the fact that they work in the realm of the unconscious, making changes at the most significant, deepest level, meaning that the more superficial elements, like attitudes, are changed too.

If you try to change your attitude, but your underpinning beliefs remain the same, the change is unlikely to last. That's like trying to move the octopus while its legs are still stuck to the rock!

You can find information on these topics and access to some great free audio files on Amanda's website http://theselfhelpbible.com/resources and we never recommend anything we haven't used, or at least thoroughly checked out, ourselves.

Getting back to your Values list, you may be surprised at your eventual top ten, but a little closer inspection can often reveal a great deal about your success rates to date.

In this instance we are talking about your career and work related success, so imagine that your top three values don't have anything to do with money. If the top three things that are important to you in a work context are all non-financial, how much chance do you think you have of making lots of money? This is such a common thing too!

The top three to five on the list show you the areas where you put your focus and attention at work. If you have a list something like:

1) Fun

2) Team work

3) Honesty

4) Fairness

5) Reward

The chances are that working with you will be nice for other people, that they will feel valued by you and that you are trustworthy, but you are unlikely to make a fortune because so many other things are more important to you.

Conversely, if money is your number one value, you will compromise everything else in order to get it. That includes things like your health and free time and other people.

Why? Because your values will filter your experience so that you only notice the things that match up with them and you will be so motivated by the things at the top that it will seem like the most normal, and correct, thing in the world. You can find more on the unconscious filtering system at work in your mind in Volume 3 of The Self Help Bible.

As with everything in life, it's a question of balance, and a realisation of your current values is a great springboard for change.

If your values already look like they will support you in your journey into entrepreneurship, then great! If not, as with just about anything in life, you can change them.

Lots of coaches have expertise in value alignment, which is all about getting your values to support your goals. If however you don't want to go as far as investing in professional help now, there are things you can do for yourself to change a value that is not serving you.

Having completed the values list, you will understand what your current unconscious values are and you will be in a great position to begin thinking about what you would rather they be and create some affirmations to help embed the idea in your unconscious.

In the third column on your sheet, write down the 'T' equivalent of each 'A' value you found in your list. Carry it on a little card with you and read it several times a day and leave it somewhere you can see it if possible. Write down what this new value will give you, as that will help with your motivation levels. Each time you catch yourself thinking in the usual way, correct yourself and remind yourself why it would serve you better to think differently. One of the prime functions of your unconscious is to serve you, so it won't take long for the new way of thinking to become a habit – as long as you consistently practice the 'new way.'

Most importantly of all, create a really juicy goal for yourself. One which is so compelling that you are champing at the bit to get to it. If you would like some help to do that, Amanda has written a book on the subject. You can find out more about it at http://theselfhelpbible.com/the-self-help-bible-books/goal-setting

Employment - The 20th Century Illusion

"We are living in a very different world today than we were just a decade ago. We're at the beginning of a whole new time... we are no longer in the Industrial Age; we are in the 'Ideas Economy' and everything has changed" Daniel Priestley

Let's have a look at why the conventional developed world life model works so well for the majority of people. What does it provide that is so fundamental that it overrides our innate curiosity and keeps us sweet? And if you are looking to change your way of life, what do you need to ensure you replace if you are going to be successful?

Centuries ago you would have known from birth your 'station in life', it was predetermined. Whether you were the gentry above stairs, or the servant below, you'd have accepted it as being your fate and just got on with it, accepting it was never going to change.

Nowadays, in the world of post industrialisation and freedom of choice, we like to think ourselves altogether more evolved and empowered, but are we really or is this all just part of an elaborate deception?

Why do the vast majority of us still spend our formative years wanting to be a fireman or a nurse, an astronaut or an air hostess? Why do we dream of growing up and going to an office wearing a nice suit and having aspirations of just enough money to buy a fast car and a big house? We grow up, for the most part, longing to conform.

We picture ourselves from a young age, growing into a replica of some successful idol – perhaps wanting to be like our parents or perhaps vowing not to be like them – either way, we rarely question the fact that we will finish our education and go and get a job for someone else, until the state says we don't have to anymore and then we'll retire when we're too old and tired to really enjoy the benefit of the money that we've worked hard for maybe 50 years to get.

And for most of us, we don't even really mind. That's how it was for our parents and how it will be for our children.

That's just how it is.

If we are really 'lucky', we may get a job that will make us seem worthy and important to other people, so that when they ask 'So, what do you do?' we can proudly answer 'I'm a brain surgeon', or 'I manage the finance division for a large multinational corporation', and they'll nod sagely and approve of us and we can feel good about ourselves.

A little less fortunate and we may end up with one of 'those' jobs that makes 'that' question sound loaded and makes us feel as though we are unable to look the other person in the eye, for fear that we might see reflected the shame and disappointment we feel inside.

Why? Because we have allowed ourselves to be pigeonholed according to what we do to earn our wages . We even refer to it as earning our *living* – even our language has evolved to imprison us. Living is our birth right, given to us by our parents. We don't earn the right to live by working for someone else!

This is all part of the illusion that we've all bought into. We have allowed ourselves to be defined by what we do to earn money.

The Illusion Part 1

Most of us have made a judgement about someone else because of their job at some point and it's not surprising really. It's just a side effect of this great illusion.

We make unconscious associations all the time, about ourselves and about others, and the barriers and rules that these associations create are part of the fabric of our modern society.

We often use our job title as a way of describing ourselves, of defining who we are.

Too insignificant a job and you might feel ashamed and somehow diminished. You may feel inferior to the person with the big job title, the swanky office and the fat bonus. You might envy them and dislike them because of the difference their role creates in your mind without actually knowing the truth about what they do and whether or not they deserve such a reward. It's as though a better paid job makes them a better person somehow.

Too big a job and you may find yourself feeling overwhelmed, like too much responsibility rests on your shoulders and obligated to others.

Interestingly, people we know who found themselves in a position above where they expected to be, have described feeling like a fraud and being in a permanent state of anxiety, believing it to be only a matter of time before they were '**found out**'!

What strange creatures we are to doubt ourselves so much!

***

KEY QUESTIONS

Have you ever felt ashamed of your job? Afraid or embarrassed to tell someone what you do? Less important than someone else just because their job ranked above yours in the company, or had a more favourable perception?

Or have you ever judged someone else according to their role? Expected them to be less intelligent perhaps or less skilled?

***

The 20th Century has created the illusion that we are all freely choosing what we do and how we live our lives, without telling us how to make it so.

It can be true, but 'they' don't want you to know that, because if everyone suddenly decided to do their own thing and live their life according to their own free will, there would be chaos.

We are not writing this book to incite anarchy or to make you dissatisfied with your life. We simply want to show you, that there in an alternative and you have the right to choose.

If you are happy to be an employee all your working life, then thank goodness for you, because the world needs employees.

If you are not though, there is another option and that's what the mindset shift is all about. Making the shift from being an employee to being an entrepreneur.

The Illusion Part 2

As human beings, we are the result of the mixture of our social conditioning and our innate instincts and drives. Some elements are primal, others are learnt and absorbed from our environment and almost all of them are deeply unconscious.

However different and individual we might like to think we are, we all have basic human needs, common to us all and the 20th Century employers have very cleverly crafted the positions they offer us as employees to cater for these needs. Company benefits, salaries related to the *'cost of living'*, pension schemes, private health care, the list goes on and in many ways it can be argued that employment does fulfil a very necessary part in society. We are not denying that. Once again our message is simply that it is <u>not the only way</u> to cater for your needs. That is the deception.

Society has come to think that we have to have a job, to work for someone else in order to thrive or at least to survive.

If you are reading this and feel like it makes sense to you, then you are one of a growing number of people who are starting to question this rationale. People are beginning to ask themselves if there is another way and thankfully, for those with the courage and conviction to dare to do something about it, there is.

Perhaps you have always felt a little different to the people around you? A bit more curious, or eager to question and explore? A bit less willing to accept everything you've been told at face value and to settle for a little life?

Let's explore this a little by taking a look at some of our human needs, our drives or instincts, because these are the things that motivate us. This will help give you a better understanding of why being an employee often feels like the safest and most secure option and begin to build a picture of what you should incorporate into a new, empowered and successful way of life as a home business entrepreneur.

Identifying Your Needs

"We are driven by five genetic needs: survival, love and belonging, power, freedom, and fun". William Glasser

As with any psychological concept, there is a great deal of debate around the fine detail of this, so we're using the categories proposed by the famous American psychologist Abraham Maslow in his 'Hierarchy of Needs'. This model is still used by many successful organisations today as a basis for HR policy, to ensure that their workforce remain satisfied and therefore loyal and is a good way to illustrate our point and hopefully make you think.

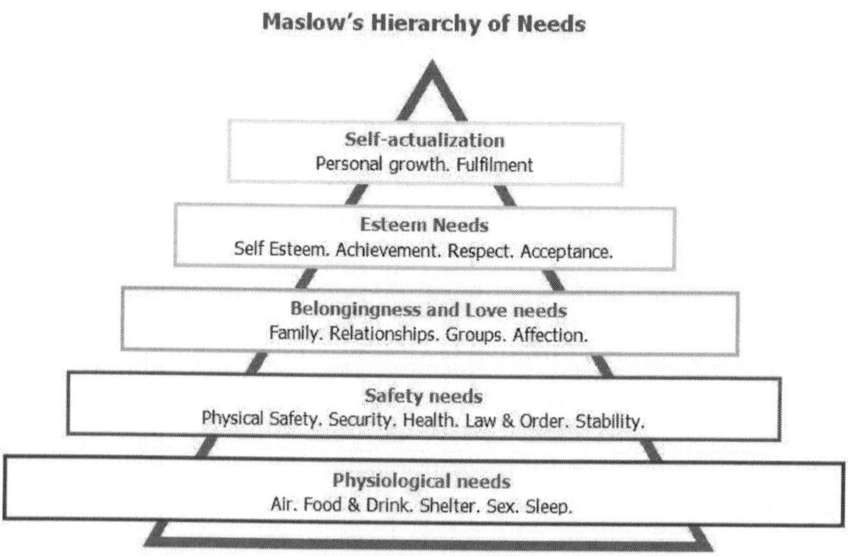

Maslow asserted that we have a range of needs which must be fulfilled in order for us to thrive and he said that they were hierarchical, some being more vital than others. For Maslow, the ultimate aim was 'Self Actualisation' or achieving your full potential in whatever area is most important to you.

In order to do this, he said that you must first achieve success in the lower levels. It is only when the lower order physical and emotional well-being needs are satisfied that we become concerned with the higher order needs of influence and personal development.

In the same way, if the things that satisfy our lower order needs are suddenly lost, our focus will revert to them and will no longer be on our higher needs. Think of it like a building; you need solid foundations before you can build walls, walls before you can add windows and windows before you can finally add curtains (or blinds if you prefer!)

If the walls fall down, your curtains will suddenly seem very unimportant won't they!

As you read through the following section, write down ways in which your current job meets your needs

Physiological and Biological Needs

The first level of his hierarchy, physiological needs is fairly self explanatory. This is the foundation of our lives and is all about survival.

We need things like food and water, air and sleep to stay alive and the sexual urge for reproduction ensures our survival as a race. When we are deprived of one or more of these needs, we are liable to go to extreme measures to secure a supply. This is what you might call our survival instinct.

If this level is not taken care of, you are unlikely to progress any further. How can you think of anything else if your most basic survival is not secure?

You might consider that exercise and stimulation of the mind cater for this level; trying to ensure that you are as physiologically and biologically well as you can be.

If you have ever been hungry, or homeless, as many highly successful home business entrepreneurs have been, you will know that it is difficult to contemplate anything other than how you are going to eat or keep warm. Even if you are lucky enough never to have experienced these things first hand, it does not take great imagination to understand why you would be preoccupied with them does it? Can you remember a time when you were hungry or cold? They are both very unpleasant and all consuming sensations aren't they; all you can think about is getting warm or eating!

Clearly a regular income contributes to this most basic level of need!

***

KEY QUESTIONS

How does your current job cater for this need?

What does it provide which caters for your physiological and biological needs either directly or indirectly?

Let's explain for example - you might not think about it but your income puts a roof over your head and feeds you and your family.

***

Safety Needs

Safety needs on the next level are perhaps not as apparent as you may at first think.

Aside from the obvious issue of physical safety, personal and financial security and health and well-being also fall under the umbrella of safety needs.

Job security (if there is such a thing nowadays) can clearly be seen to respond to this need; having the steady and reliable income afforded you by a stable, conventional job. This is definitely something you will want to recreate in your new career as an entrepreneur and a good reason to ensure that you do not try to run before you can walk. If you make the leap into a new way of earning your living without proper investigation, preparation and planning you may find yourself unable to provide for this basic need and you will soon find yourself gravitating back to what you previously did to fulfil this need.

That's why we always suggest, if possible, getting started alongside your current job/employment.

Remember that when you are frightened you will always tend to shrink back into the relative safety and familiarity of your comfort zone. If you suddenly aren't earning enough money, that's a sure fire way to scare yourself!

That's one reason why it is often best to make the move from employee to full time home business entrepreneur in stages. Build up your new income streams until they are well established enough to support you and then cross over. If you throw in your job too early, you introduce all kinds of additional internal and external pressures which may ruin your chances. Remember, this is a lifestyle change you are thinking of making here. It's not the same as just changing jobs.

Things like procedures, laws and rules are created to cater for this level of need - they reassure and protect you. HR policies to protect you from unfair or unjust treatment and a healthcare system to take care of your physical and mental well being are also familiar examples.

The desire to have some money saved for 'a rainy day' would arise from this need for security. Insurance policies might be seen to exploit this human need or to respond to it depending on your point of view!

***

KEY QUESTIONS

How does your current job cater for this need?

What does it provide which caters for your need for safety and security either directly or indirectly?

Is there anything which makes you feel vulnerable or unsafe? The veiled threat of job loss is a very common example, particularly in a recession.

***

Love and Belonging

"By building relations we create a source of love and personal pride and belonging that makes living in a chaotic world easier." Susan Lieberman

Stemming from our primeval herding instinct, where we grouped together in order to survive, the next category in Maslow's hierarchy is linked to interpersonal needs and our desire to belong. This encompasses the world of feelings and in particular our need to feel like we belong and are accepted.

The need to belong can sometimes be so strong that it overrides our need for safety and even our physiological needs. People with eating disorders may ignore the need for food in order to fit in with peers for example, or to conform to the societal image of how they should look to be beautiful. It is very common for people to stay in an abusive or unhappy relationship rather than find themselves alone.

Have you ever gone against your own opinion or values in order to 'tow the company line'? Kept quiet when you could have spoken out just to avoid being the odd one out? Worked extra hours to be well seen at work at perhaps considerable personal cost?

Previously, our family and close community would have taken care of this need, but we don't tend to live in real communities anymore and cross generational family living is rare now. Instead people find acceptance and a sense of belonging from joining groups, clubs and societies, from taking part in social, sporting or religious activities and especially at work - perhaps unsurprising given the amount of time you actually spend there!

Gangs evolve to cater for this need, even self help groups where people gather together to share their experience of a common problem. We find love and acceptance when we feel similar to others.

You're probably familiar with the term 'rapport'. We talk about having a good rapport with someone we like and feel we have things in common with. Rapport is simply a connection at an unconscious level which fools us into thinking the other person is like us and therefore at this level at least, we like them. We are hard wired to like people we believe are like us.

When this need is neglected at a formative age, people may have difficulty forming and maintaining emotional relationships throughout their lives.

Unfulfilled in later life, even those who have had a healthy and complete upbringing, may feel lonely, isolated and tend towards depression.

It is a common misconception that leaving the familiar community of employment will mean being isolated and lonely. Let us reassure you now, that it doesn't have to! You can meet lots of like minded and supportive people if you know where to look and what to beware of. Look us up on Facebook if you want to find some like minded people. You can find our contact details at the end of the book.

***

KEY QUESTIONS

How does your current job cater for this need?

What does it provide which caters for your need to feel love and belonging, either directly or indirectly?

What does it do that contradicts or denies this need?

***

Esteem

For Maslow, esteem falls into two areas, the need to be respected and accepted by others and the need to respect yourself – Self Esteem.

We believe having a good, solid sense of self; a foundation of self esteem on which to build is vital. It's part of the reason we've spent a lot of time and money on our own personal development.

We all need to feel that we are competent and make a meaningful contribution in some way and this may be through hobbies and activities, in our relationships with others or through our work.

As we now typically spend longer at work, the need for recognition and acceptance is often fulfilled through our jobs. You may base your self-worth and value on the feedback and opinion of others and if you don't get enough to make you feel secure, you may either go to more extreme lengths to get it, or feel unhappy.

Some people will resort to outrageous or exaggerated behaviour in order to draw attention to themselves. Unless they have good self esteem however, the acceptance of others is not enough; this is not an 'either-or' scenario. This is why personal development is so important. You cannot be successful and happy if you do not have healthy self esteem. Many very rich people are unhappy and this stems from an internal conflict, which means that in some way they are unable to accept that they deserve to be wealthy.

Conversely, some people are very happy without being rich, they will have great levels of healthy self-esteem!

One thing which is quite strange once you think about it, is that often we don't really like the people we work with and yet we happily (or rather unhappily) take their feelings about us to heart as though they were gold.

***

KEY QUESTIONS

How does your current job cater for this need?

What does it give you which contributes to your needs for good levels of esteem?

What does it do that contradicts or denies this need?

Of all the people you work with, how many of them do you really like?

Would you choose to spend time with many of them? And of those you wouldn't, do you allow their opinions or behaviour to affect how you feel?

If so WHY? Can you identify the fear which underlies this behaviour?

***

Self-actualization

"A musician must make music, an artist must paint, a poet must write, if he is to be ultimately at peace with himself. What a man can be, he must be. He must be true to his own nature. This need we may call self-actualization."
Abraham Maslow

Maslow described self-actualized people as those who were fulfilled and doing all they were capable of and this level is all about our perceived need to reach our potential. More specific in its detail than the other levels, it will be different for each person.

We might want to be recognised as the authors of a best-selling book, as great mentors, or as having inspired others, you might want to be the next Steve Jobs or Richard Branson, to paint beautiful pictures or write great music. The permutations are as endless as the drops of water in the sea.

Maslow believed that only once you had accomplished the lower orders, would you be able to achieve the last desire for self actualisation.

***

KEY QUESTIONS

What do you think?

Do you need to reach satisfactory levels in the areas at the bottom of the pyramid in order to reach the top, or can you simply jump the levels in between?

How close do you think you are to self actualisation?

What would have to change in your life in order for you to achieve self actualisation?

What will self actualisation mean for you?

***

It's interesting that this level, is perhaps in some regards the most important level in terms of satisfaction and yet the least likely to be fulfilled by your job!

This is the level that takes you beyond your existence, sees you achieving your potential and doing the things that you are passionate about. If you got paid to do this you would never feel like you were working again!

Whether you whole heartedly agree with Maslow's classifications or not is irrelevant, what is undeniably clear to see, is that our jobs cater for many needs other than just financial ones. Of course the money is important, we cannot comfortably exist in the modern world without at least some, but the money is only a vehicle, a means to an end.

When we say we want more money, what we actually mean is much deeper than that. It's not even about the things we can buy with more money, it's about the feelings that those things can give us, the choices that open up to us as a result.

Your Job and Your Needs

It is important to acknowledge all the positive purposes that your job serves, so that you can ensure that your new career as a home business entrepreneur will fill the gaps left behind when you make the shift.

It is also important to highlight the areas which a new way of earning money could improve. This gives you a quantifiable start-point for your journey and a clear picture of what you are going to improve upon.

If you are not currently employed, please answer the questions with your most recent/significant job in mind or whatever feels like the right thing to you.

***

Exercise

1) Taking each of Maslow's headings as a start point, list all the ways your job fulfils these needs. You can use the questions listed in the 'The Key Question's' sections.

2) List how you think your new career might also take care of these needs. If there are any you are not yet sure of, highlight them so that you can be aware that you'll need to find a solution.

3) What needs did your last job not satisfactorily fulfil and why? Were there any of Maslow's levels it didn't cater for at all?

If so, was this due to the nature of the job, a short coming of the organisation, or something more personal – a lack of knowledge or willingness on your part for example? Be honest, this is only for you and the better picture you have, the clearer the way ahead will be. If you're going to be your own boss it's useless pretending to be the ideal employee!

4) What aspects of your job made you feel good?

5) What elements did you enjoy doing?

6) What aspects of your job made you feel unhappy?

7) What elements did you not enjoy?

8) On a scale of 1 to 10, where 10 is the best, how satisfied were you with your job?

9) If you had to pick one word, to describe the way you feel about your job what would it be?

10) Now pick a word to describe how you would love to feel about your job. Write it down.

What Will You Give?

"It had long since come to my attention that people of accomplishment rarely sat back and let things happen to them. They went out and happened to things" Leonardo da Vinci

Having decided what you want to get out, you also need to think about, and be very clear on, what you are prepared to put into this lifestyle change.

What are you willing to invest? Time? Money? It may be that you have little of one or the other, or both, but unless you are prepared to invest some of each you are not going to be successful as a home business entrepreneur.

You cannot start a new business without some cost being involved and without having to learn some new things along the way. That's a big clue to the validity of these things you see online, that tell you you can make a six figure income with no investment and working 2 hours a week!

Think how much time you currently invest at work, even if you are in a job and so don't have to pay for it. The important thing here is to be realistic and the rule of thumb, if it seems to good to be true it probably is, was never truer than online!

You will have to spend time and money if you want to build a successful business.

But, it doesn't have to be so much of either that it cripples you in the meantime. There are some really great businesses with low start up costs that allow you to learn at your own pace and even to earn as you learn. Just do it at the speed that's right for you. Start with a little time and a small investment, so that you can do it alongside your existing career and then you don't have the added pressure of needing immediate success. Then as your new business grows, you can make a comfortable transition, confident that you are going to be successful. Starting out this way you'll be growing lovely strong legs for your octopus too!

Being open to learning is another really key point. As well as investing time and money in your business, you need to be prepared to invest in your own learning and development.

Every successful business person we know spends, or has spent considerable time and money on their own development. That might be reading books, watching videos, listening to audios, getting a coach or mentor, attending live events – the choice is yours but remember this –

Your best thinking to date has got you to where you are today. If you want to go further, do better, get more you need to do something differently.

What Have You Already Got?

Let's assume that your life is not a complete disaster. Before you say,

"Well mine is"

We know the old adage about what happens when you assume! (You make an '*ass*' out of '*u*' and '*me*' – you've probably heard that too!) But we like taking calculated risks, and we're basing this assumption on the fact that wherever you currently are in your life, you are reading this book, so you obviously haven't given up and

If you haven't given up, then you haven't failed.

You've got this far doing things one way and you need to recognise that as an achievement in itself. Not *everything* in your life is a disaster – even if it feels that way sometimes.

Equally important as deciding where you want to go next and what you need to change, you also need to work out what's worth keeping.

What are your strengths?

What's worked well in your current job?

What will you keep and what will you leave behind?

If you've followed the exercises up to this point, you should already have a better idea of what's important to you in the context of your work (your values) and what you need your job to provide for you (your needs)

You should also understand what has kept you content where you are until now, because certain elements will be vital to your future success.

***

Exercise

Albert S Humphrey devised a great tool called the SWOT Matrix during the1960s, perfect for analysing what sort of business would align best with your talents.

The basic premise is this.

SWOT stands for Strengths, Weaknesses, Opportunities and Threats.

To carry out a SWOT analysis, you need to first draw up a chart like the one below. You can download an example at http://theselfhelpbible.com/resources/worksheets

Strengths	**Weaknesses**
What do you do well? What unique resources do you have access to? What do others see as your strengths?	What could you improve? Where do you have less resources than others? What are others likely to see as your weaknesses?
Opportunities	**Threats**
What opportunities are open to you? What trends could you take advantage of? How can you turn your strengths into opportunities?	What threats could harm you? What is your competition doing? What threats do your weaknesses expose you to?

List your attributes and areas for improvement in the top two boxes labelled 'Strengths' and 'Weaknesses'. Then in the bottom two, you can list opportunities that will be available to you thanks to your strengths, and threats that you need to be aware of.

You'll notice that the top two are mainly internal ideas and the bottom two external. This raises an important question. Who do you look to, to know that you've done a good job? If you are looking to other, external sources, this is another reason to be careful who you choose to work with and who to listen to.

If you're not sure, just answer this – how do you know when you've done a good job? Does someone else have to tell you, or do you just know?

If someone else has to tell you, you operate with an external frame of reference. If you just know, your reference frame is internal. Either is fine, just be aware of yours and the fact that it's one of the unconscious filters we talked about earlier.

If you have an internal frame of reference and poor self belief, or an external frame and unpleasant people giving you feedback, you are going to doubt and question yourself a lot. In all cases, good self belief and solid self esteem are key!

When you come to size up a business, you can do a similar analysis on it and quickly see if it will be a good fit for you.

If you need help identifying what your strengths and weaknesses are, try looking at your performance reviews and personal objectives at work, have a chat with your boss, speak to your HR team about having some kind of skills analysis or personality profiling done, or ask a friend who you trust well enough to give you an honest answer – warts and all! Don't be afraid to ask your current employer's help with this assessment, most organisations welcome personal development and if they have some kind of development policy in place, you may even help them fulfil some of their objectives. You just might want to refrain from telling them you're trying to work out what to take with you when you leave them!

Dealing With Crabs!

"Care about what other people think and you will always be their prisoner". Lao Tzu

An unusual title in a book about mindset perhaps, but crabs are a real hazard when you are looking at making change in your life and stepping beyond the boundaries of normality!

Did you go crabbing when you were a child? Catching crabs with a piece of bacon tied to the end of a string and collecting them in a bucket full of sea water? If so you may well remember their predictable behaviour too.

The first crab would hog the bacon all to himself, even if it were twice his size, and defend it viciously, hitting out at the others who joined him in the bucket with his claws, and stuffing as much in his mouth as he could. All the others would crowd round and try to steal his haul.

After a while, one crab would try and escape from the bucket, often climbing on top of those still fighting for food at the bottom, and just as he was making real progress, another crab would grab his legs and pull him back down into the water, increasing the number competing for the same grotty bit of bacon by one. It was rare that one ever escaped because his fellow crabs would pull him back down into the mêlée of more conventional crab like behaviour.

When you decide to change your life and to make the mindset shift, you will suddenly find yourself surrounded by crabs.

Friends, family, colleagues and all sorts of well wishers, will suddenly want to swing off your legs, offer you the benefit of their opinion and pull you right back down into the bucket!

Don't let them!

Remember that they have grown up under the same conditions as you, and that you are the one about to break free from the dreaded 'norm'. Their mindset is very firmly set on the traditional model of work for someone else all your life and that's great: FOR THEM.

That doesn't mean it's great for you. Do not allow them to dissuade you from your new path.

The best way we have found to deal with this, is to keep in mind that most of the time, they genuinely do have your best interests at heart – but it's their version of what your best interests are and that's the key.

Their concern comes from a good place - and even if you suspect it doesn't, choose to believe it does. It allows you to feel good in yourself and to continue to think well of them. Thinking negatively about them means having negative thoughts in your mind, which your unconscious will take personally and which will cloud your mind. So believe they want what's right for you, they just can't know what that is because they aren't you.

Step two is to not engage with them about what you are doing. This can be tricky if it's your partner or parent but if you don't talk much about it, neither will they. Yes it might lead them to think you've joined a cult, but so what!

Just as you need to remember that you have the right to your way of doing things, you also need to remember that they do too. Avoid trying to 'win them round' or 'get them on board'. Just get on with building a successful life for yourself and later, your example will be the best selling tool you have if you do want any of them to join you.

It really boils down to mutual respect. Respect their choice to disagree with your way of doing things and in time they will likely do the same, and if they don't, well that's up to them.

Remember, no other person can make you feel anything unless you choose to. They may know how to appeal to your good nature or manipulate you into feeling a particular way, but only if you let them. You have the absolute power over your emotions, you may have forgotten that fact or never learnt it well enough to use it properly, but this is just part of the enormous power that you posses and can use if you choose to.

Here are some of the most common reasons why people around you will suddenly behave like crabs!

Some will try to hold you back because unconsciously they don't want you to do better than them.

Some because being a home business entrepreneur is outside of their sphere of reference and they can't comprehend it. We have a tendency to stick with what we know – that comfort zone blanket again!

Some because they tried something else and it didn't work for them. They won't want to contemplate that it might work for you for all the same reasons. Remember that there are hundreds of thousands of people already doing what you want to do, they're just not yet in your entourage.

Some out of concern for you that you might fail. They might not want you to be hurt or disappointed - or they may just want to avoid the potential fallout!

Some because if you are successful, it might call their own way of doing things into question and if they're not ready for that, they aren't going to want you holding that mirror up to them are they!

Whatever their reasons, they are <u>their</u> reasons. You may have to toughen up for a while but it will be worth it! This is another reason why you need to be really clear what your motivation is. If you are clear why you are doing this, their pincers will just slide off your shell no matter how hard they might try to pull you back into the bucket!

The people around you will have a big impact on you, whatever you decide to do in life. Even if you decide that actually, you prefer to stick with what you already know and the relative security or your familiar job, you should still pay attention to who you spend time with.

Think about someone you know who is prone to be a bit of a moaner, a drama queen, or a martyr, don't you find that after a while in their company you feel drained and fed up? We call these people mood-hoovers because they literally suck the life out of you!

It's a proven fact that the most successful people in any area, spend most of their time with other successful people. If you want to be a millionaire, find a way to get to know some of them. If you want to be a better salesman, spend some time with people who are brilliant salesmen (or women). Success leaves clues, and by spending time in their company you are bound to pick some up, even if you don't want to go as far as deliberately trying to work out what makes them tick.

Avoid negative, narrow minded people and instead elect to spend more time in the company of people who inspire you, lift you up and make you laugh. Your unconscious is like a sponge and will soon soak up the vibes, or moods around you.

Think of your life like a garden and fill it with beautiful flowers, interesting plants and nourishing fruits. The weeds can grow elsewhere!

The Shocking Truth

You may have seen lots of promises online for systems that will make you rich while you sleep, without you having to do anything at all. If this is how you plan to finance your future, then you might want to sit down for this next bit.

Don't believe everything you see and hear online.

We're sorry to have to tell you this, but they don't work and anyone that tells you that you can get rich without an investment on your part is lying to you. The investment will be time and some money and it will definitely involve learning and implementing. Whatever, you need to accept and commit there will be an investment. Without it, your business will go nowhere.

This may come as a shock, but some people online tell lies! Just as there are people in the real world who can't be trusted, so there are people in the virtual world you should steer clear of too.

Due diligence is ever more important. Before signing up for anything, with anybody, do your homework.

Research as much as you can on the people and products and be very cautious. Find someone you feel you can trust. Speak to them in person if you can, get to know them before giving them your time, money and ideas.

***

Amanda's Story

When I first started working online, I was so excited and as usual took the people I met at face value. I value my integrity very highly and expect other people to be honest too.

The net result was that I lost a lot of money in exchange for a system that I didn't understand and never got to grips with, and needless to say, didn’t make a penny with.

Undeterred, I went and did a very similar thing again, this time spending even more money for a more simple system that I could understand and after lots of hours of hard work, I made… Wait for it… Nothing.

In both cases I'd made errors of judgement and given money to people who couldn't be trusted. Interestingly both continue to work online to this day, though not with the systems they sold me!

This was a tough lesson but one well learnt and now I get to help you avoid the same mistake, so it wasn't in vain.

What I didn't do in either case was ask for some proper proof of the systems or research the people. I did actually meet one of them and he reminded me of some dodgy second hand car sales man! He'd had my money by then though so it was a bit late!

It won't always be possible to meet people, the internet makes the world a very small place but only in a virtual sense, but you can get a feel for them by seeing who they are friends with, where they are online and what people say about them. Do a bit of digging and take enough time to weigh up your options. Get to know them on Facebook or whichever social media platform you prefer, see how they interact with others and you'll soon begin to get a picture. If they are genuine they'll have no problem with you wanting to be sure and won't try and rush you into making decisions.

The only note of caution is to be clear about your own motives. Procrastination is something many of us are good at and we hide it behind many smoke screens. Due diligence is important, do enough to be sure but don't wait forever and use this as an excuse to procrastinate! There's a balance, find yours by being really honest with yourself and doing the first steps outlined here, working out what you want and what you're prepared to do to get it. Then make a decision. If you don't make that decision, again, your business will not succeed.

Tools to Help You Focus

"The secret of change is to focus all of your energy, not on fighting the old, but on building the new". Socrates

We use lots of tools to help keep us on track. Some of them may suit you better than others and you may have some more of your own to add. You don't have to use them all, but these are a few we've tried between us and would recommend. We are not going into the detail of how to use them all here, but you can find more information and tools to help you at http://www.theselfhelpbible.com

* Dream boards

* Visualisation

* Affirmations

* Subliminal messaging

* Hypnosis

* Goal Setting

* Reading inspirational and motivational books

* Watching inspirational videos

* Meeting like minded people

* Keeping a journal

* Thinking – we spend a lot of time thinking!

* Meditation

* Attending personal development workshops or seminars

Some Simple Dos and Don'ts

Things we've learnt along the way...

You must do your due diligence. There are lots of online 'gurus', and 'experts' who aren't really anything of the sort. Take time to find out about the system you are looking at and the people you'd be working with if your business involves working with others. There are some really reputable sites where you can get sound reviews about online systems and people who are sharks will get found out in the end, so read around. Try to talk to them in person if you can. Anyone who claims to offer mentoring or coaching of any description will be willing to talk to you before they work with you and if they won't, then you are unlikely to get much support from them later so stay clear.

Sites like Facebook can also be a good place to get a feel for what someone is like. You will make your own judgements, but as a rule of thumb, if someone doesn't have a real picture on Facebook, we don't tend to connect with them. We are in the business of helping people and expect a level of commitment and honesty – cartoons and generic images don't say that to us, so we tend to steer clear – but that's just one of our measures.

You can also see what a person is like from the things they display on their walls. If you find a pattern of things which offend you in some way, then you are unlikely to be happy bed fellows. That's no more a statement about them than it is about you, but if you are building your own business, then choose who to include carefully that's all.

Choose to work with someone you like, you trust, feel you can work with, is accessible

Don't be put off by their story just because it's different to yours – see beyond their why, you have your own, but see if their system is right for you

Don't be reeled in by their story either – pity is not a reason to go into business with someone.

Don't be fooled by things like income screen shots – they can be easily faked. If we had a dollar for every screen shot we'd seen since we've been online, we'd be multi-millionaires! When you're new to the technological world, it can be dazzling, but just because you can see it doesn't mean it's real! Think super models and spots. When you see them in a photograph when they've been 'papped' – no makeup and bed hair – they look very different to when they've been airbrushed and photo-shopped don't they! Bank statements and affiliate sales income sheets are no different! Not all of them are fake though, again it comes down to a question of due diligence and being discerning – as with anything in life.

Don’t invest in something that compromises your core values e.g. if being alone and self sufficient is important to you in a work context, investing in a business where you will need to network and build a group is not going to work for you.

Similarly, don't pick something that relies on doing something you hate. For example, if you hate the idea of face to face sales meetings, don’t invest in a business that requires it.

Don’t invest in something you don't believe in. If you don’t believe in it; neither will anyone else you try to tell about it. You'll project your own lack of belief and it'll be all the cue those crabs need to grab you by the legs and pull you down!

Find something you will enjoy doing. They say if you can make your passion your job, you will never work another day, and it's true. We do what we love now and even though it might mean late nights and long hours sometimes, it never feels like working for someone else did!

Find the system, programme, business that matches up with what you want to do and is flexible enough to allow you to do it your way. That's why we love our blogging platform and business so much. We can use it as a vehicle for whatever we want to do.

Find something you can imagine telling your best friend about without being afraid of sounding stupid. If you can find something that excites you and you feel secure about, you will go into it with more confidence and self belief, expecting success before you start. This will increase your chances of success immeasurably.

Don't succumb to ADOS. '*Attention Deficit – Oooh, Shiny!* '

If you are looking online, there are always things to catch your eye and lead you off somewhere else. If you are going to be working online, you'll probably be looking to make your own versions! If you are looking for something, restrict yourself to what you are looking at. Switch off distractions like Facebook and keep your sessions to time slots that match your focus length. Anything longer and you'll just drift off and end up wasting valuable time.

Use what you already know. Don't reinvent the wheel if you don't have to. If you know what you are good at and what you enjoy, incorporate them into your new business. Finding new ways to knit things together may well give you a new spin that makes your business unique, so think boldly and creatively.

Be open to opportunity. Things don't always come packaged in the way you might expect, so stay open minded and look beyond the obvious. If you wait for the perfect moment, when everything is just as you imagined it would be, you may well miss the boat. You are limited by your imagination to a degree, so don't dismiss something that you couldn't have imagined out of hand.

Look back over your life, and chances are you'll find at least one example of a time when things didn't turn out the way you expected. Something that you were disappointed in or didn't welcome at the time, may well have turned out to be a blessing in disguise with hindsight.

Remember, an oyster looks just like a grotty shell from the outside, but within there may well be a pearl!

Chris and Susan's Story

We are both from a professional background as accountants and management consultants and have owned and run our own businesses since 1983, so making a change from the traditional "*time for money*" way of life was as much a change for us, as it most likely is for you as you are reading this.

The seed was sown ten years ago when we discovered network marketing and came to understand that there were alternative ways to make money other than the traditional job income. Whilst our first foray into that market was not as successful in monetary terms as we expected, what we learnt forms the basis of our business today - principally the importance of leverage and building a residual income. The same formula that the most prosperous people in the world use to create their wealth - people like Robert Kiyosaki and Donald Trump to name but a few.

Fast forward to 2009, in our fifties, we realised that time was marching on, the children had left home and we hadn't yet achieved our dream to travel the world and especially to spend a whole season pursuing our passion of skiing (everyone has to have a reason why). We knew that if we continued to "**work**" our management consultancy, the only way we could generate more income was to work longer hours and that wasn't going to happen!

Long story short - we don't have a '*rags to riches*' story; we have not been addicted to alcohol or drugs, been homeless or anything like that - but one particular event in our business led us to know that we had to make a change in our lives if we were to '*live our dream*'. It will be the same for you.

As a result of that event we set about researching a way that we could do that. A way which would fulfil our criteria - we wanted to be able to work from home, or anywhere in the world (passion for travel). This naturally led us to the internet and the decision to work online. Of course your criteria may be very different to ours, that doesn't matter, as you long as you know what your reason why is.

What a minefield that was! Everywhere you looked people appeared to be making serious amounts of money from various online business opportunities. Our challenge, just like yours was "*is it real?*", "*who can you trust?*", "*can I do it?*" We can tell you that we made some mistakes and were seduced by some very clever people hiding behind well written sales pages - what we now call 'the internet magicians'. We bought plenty of shiny objects (ADOS!), what we now famously call *'Shelf Development'* products, because they never get any further than the shelf! You will undoubtedly do the same or have done the same. We learnt from that just like Amanda did. You will learn from it as well - maybe you already have! The best advice we can give is to do what we call in accountant speak your '*due diligence*'. That means research diligently what is being offered. *Does it align with your personal values, passion or experience. Can you contact someone? Can you speak to a real person? Have they achieved the success you desire?*

We would also advise that you don't just go and quit your job; that you build your new home business part time. This gives you the financial security of knowing you have one stream of income whilst you develop another.

This is exactly what we did - so that in six months of working our management consultancy full time and building our home business online part time we were able to make the switch.

But Don't Just Take Our Word For It!

In 2012 on a rare visit to London Susan met up with Sharon Lechter who is Co-Author with Robert Kiyosaki of the 'Rich Dad Poor Dad' books and Worldwide Emissary for The Napoleon Hill Foundation. Susan asked Sharon the question

"A lot of people who are employed or never owned a business want to start their first business but have a problem stepping over the line to become an entrepreneur.

What would you say to them to help them take that next step?"

This is what Sharon said in response

"If your life and wealth require a guaranteed income don't quit your job outright but start going to seminars; start looking at what it is you want to do as a business and start getting involved... learn about what you want to do so you gain knowledge because once you understand more about what you want to start a business around a lot of that FEAR will go away. You can start your business on the side and then all of a sudden you are going to see that your part time business is making more and more money and you can say goodbye to your employment but without that fear, without putting yourself or your family at risk.

Understand what that risk is to you and acknowledge it but also know you are doing what's right for your family - take a step by step transition.

Stay as an employee and start a business on the side. Keep reading ... Surround yourself with people already in that business so that you can learn from them because ***successful people want to help others to become successful****..."*

http://TheMindsetShift.com/SharonLechter

Very wise words indeed and words that we endorse in this book because it very much follows what we did.

Last but not least...

Invest not just in the tools and resources for your home business but in your lifelong personal development and training that makes your business the best it can be. Feed your mind by reading books, listening to audios, CD's, MP3's and of course materials that contribute to your positive mindset - just like this book you are reading now.

"A man is but the product of his thoughts. What he thinks he becomes" Henry Ford

Make sure you hang out and associate with positive people and you will soon find you attract others just like you into your life and your business.

"Surround yourself with only people who are going to lift you higher" Oprah Winfrey

...and Lastly

You've reached the end of what we have written for you here. We hope very sincerely, that you have enjoyed it and found some tools that will give you the confidence to forge ahead in your quest to become a home business entrepreneur.

One of the hardest things in writing this, believe it or not, has been deciding what to leave out! We wanted to arm you with enough to start your journey, without overwhelming you and so have kept the book intentionally short. We hope you think that was a good decision.

All the other things that we thought about including, you will find appearing on our websites and Facebook pages, so do please connect with us there too. We'd love to be able to walk the road with you a little longer.

To sum up, we'd simply like to say, your current mindset has got you as far as you've come; if you want to go further you are going to have to make some changes. They don't have to be big or scary, but they will transform your life.

Begin by working out what your WHY is, what motivates you, what you have in your life that you want to preserve and what you want to change.

That gives you the start for your journey.

Examine your own beliefs, values and fears, with regards to making money, being rich, success, your own ability and worth and anything else that you feel is important for you. Work out what they are, what you want them to be, and change them.

Be aware of who you spend your time with and what you are saying to yourself.

This removes the obstacles on the road.

Create some compelling goals and use all the tools at your disposal to help support the mindset that you need, in order to get the success you want and deserve.

This leads you and sustains you on your journey.

Finally, get ready to celebrate your success and look forward to that day in your future, when you will look back upon this moment in time and recognise it as the moment that changed your life, because that's how long it takes, just an instant.

The instant you decide and commit to make the Mindset Shift.

"Don't wait until everything is just right. It will never be perfect. There will always be challenges, obstacles, and less than perfect conditions. So what? Get started now. With each step you take, you will grow stronger and stronger, and more and more skilled, more and more self confident, and more and more successful" Mark Victor Hansen - Co-creator of the #1 New York Times best-selling series Chicken Soup for the Soul and co-author of Cracking the Millionaire Code and The One Minute Millionaire

Live with Passion & Purpose - The Secret to You

http://TheMindsetShift.com/TheSecret

Stay In Touch ...

If you've read and enjoyed our book, we'd really appreciate it if you could take a couple of minutes to post a review wherever you bought it, or on Amazon.

We'd love to hear from you too and there are lots of ways you can get in touch with us. Here are the most popular choices.

Facebook: http://www.facebook.com/Theselfhelpbible

Facebook: http://www.facebook.com/Themindsetshift

Twitter http://www.twitter.com@themindsetshift

Websites

http://www.TheSelfHelpBible.com

http://www.ChrisAndSusanBeesley.com

http://www.TheSelfHelpBible.com/MindsetShift

What Others Have Said About The Mindset Shift

Having made millions of dollars over the course of my career, the key to success lies in one's ability to visualize the future as you would like it to be...NOW. But in order to do that a shift in consciousness and awareness must take place.

The Mindset Shift provides all of the tools you will need to make that shift and give you the confidence you need to go from working for someone else, to working for yourself.

The book provides easy to implement exercises that will have you thinking outside the box within a few hours of reading it - another important factor that will either make or break you as an entrepreneur.

Highly recommended reading for anyone looking to have success with setting up their own business.

Darren Little

Millionaire Mentor

Contributing Author Chicken Soup for the Network

Marketer's Soul

Co-Author MLM Affiliate Magic

***

As you are reading this go back to a time in your life when you just believed.

I know there was a time in your life when you believed in something; it may not have made sense to others, but it made sense to you. The fire inside of you spoke out to you and whispered:

This is where you need to be. You are in the right place, right here, right now."

Take that power into the present moment, and harness the power of belief.

Read this book. Make a decision - and step into the amazing world of Home Business Entrepreneurship.

David Wood
CEO and Co-Founder Empower Network

4752662R00081

Printed in Great Britain
by Amazon.co.uk, Ltd.,
Marston Gate.